Energy for the Future

by Therese Hudson

Scott Foresman
is an imprint of

PEARSON

Glenview, Illinois • Boston, Massachusetts • Mesa, Arizona
Shoreview, Minnesota • Upper Saddle River, New Jersey

People are **consumers** of **energy**. We use energy to freeze and cook food. We use energy to heat and cool our homes. Energy lets us drive cars, use computers, and watch movies.

Right now, most people need oil to produce most of their energy. Using too much oil can be bad for Earth. It can make Earth dirty and can hurt people, animals, and plants. Also, oil on Earth will not last forever. We need to find other places to get energy.

We use energy for many things in our lives.

 energy comes from the sun. Everything on Earth needs the sun's energy to live. The sun gives off heat that warms Earth. This heat can be gathered and used in different ways. A solar water heater is one way to use the sun's energy.

A solar water heater uses the sun's energy to heat water. The heated water is held in a tank until people need to use it. Some kinds of solar water heaters work even when it is very cold outside. The water from the heater is so warm that someone could use it to take a bath!

This home uses solar energy, or energy from the sun, to heat water.

Solar energy can also be used to produce electricity. The sun heats water until it turns into steam. The steam causes the blades of a machine to turn. The turning blades produce energy that can be made into electricity.

Solar energy is a good way to produce electricity. Solar energy does not make Earth dirty. Also, since it comes from the sun, it does not cost a lot of money. We will not run out of energy from the sun.

Steam makes these blades turn.

People used energy from wind before they began using oil and gas. Wind pushed ships across the seas. People even used the wind to get water from the ground.

Today, people use the wind to produce electricity. Producing electricity from the wind is like producing electricity from the sun's heat. Instead of using heat to make steam, the wind turns the blades.

The wind turns these large blades to produce electricity.

6

A lot of electricity can be produced on a wind farm. A wind farm is a place with many blades for producing electricity. The harder the wind blows, the more electricity is produced. Wind energy can produce electricity all the time. Wind energy can produce electricity day and night.

Wind energy is a lot like solar energy. It does not make Earth dirty, and it does not cost a lot of money. We will not run out of wind energy.

There are many blades for the wind to turn on a wind farm.

Some energy comes from things that were once living. When wood from trees is burned, the energy from the wood comes out. As the energy from the wood comes out, we can see light and feel heat.

People can use the energy from many different kinds of plants. Some kinds of plants can be turned into a liquid that can be used in cars. This liquid can replace the gas used in cars, trucks, and trains.

Some people burn oil from corn to run their cars! People are testing other plants to see if they can use them in the same way. These tests will help people make **decisions** about how to use the energy from different plants.

Energy from plants can be used to power cars.

People can even use energy that comes from heat deep inside Earth. The inside of Earth is very hot. There is also a lot of water inside Earth. The heat makes the water very hot. Sometimes this hot water shoots out of Earth. When this hot water comes out, it is called a geyser (GY-zer).

The picture on this page shows Old Faithful geyser in Yellowstone National Park. The hot water that shoots out of the geyser comes from far below Earth's surface.

Hot water is trapped inside the ground in many places. People drill holes in the ground to reach that hot water. Then they use it to produce electricity.

Drilling holes in the ground can hurt animals and plants. Animals might not have a place to live. Plants might not have a place to grow. People must try not to hurt many animals and plants when they drill into the ground.

A place like this one can take hot water from inside Earth and produce electricity.

People can even use the water in rivers to produce energy. First, people build a dam. A dam is a large wall in a river that stops the water from flowing. The water gathers into a lake behind the dam. Water from the lake turns blades. The blades produce energy that can be made into electricity.

Sometimes dams can hurt animals and plants. Animals who live in the river can get trapped in the lake. Plants that grow near the river can die as the lake becomes larger. People must be careful when they build dams.

Dams can produce electricity, but they can also hurt plants and animals.

People are energy consumers. People can be **producers**, too. You might use solar energy to make your own hot water. You might use wind to make electricity for your house. You might even grow plants to power your car!

If people learn to use the different kinds of energy around us, there will be enough energy for everyone in the future.

Solar panels on rooftops

Hot and Hotter

You just read about solar energy. You learned that heat from the sun is used to make hot water. You also learned that heat from the sun can turn water into steam. This steam can be used to make electricity. But is the sun really hot enough to make steam?

Water must be 100 degrees Celsius (212 degrees Fahrenheit) to turn into steam. Special machines and other things can help make the sun's heat even hotter. Now it is your turn to see how black paper can help make the sun even hotter!

Follow the five steps on page 15 to see how black paper can help make the sun even hotter.

1. Get two similar thermometers. Cover the bulb of one thermometer with black paper.

2. Look at the temperature of both thermometers. Write down the temperatures.

3. Put both thermometers in the sun. Wait ten minutes.

4. Look at the temperature of both thermometers again. Write down the new temperatures.

5. Tell how the temperatures of the thermometers changed.

Glossary

consumers *n.* users of products

decisions *n.* choices

energy *n.* power

producers *n.* makers of products

solar *adj.* from the sun